YOUR KNOWLEDGE HAS VALUE

Mark Schauer

Native Genocide and American Imperialism in Simon Ortiz's poem "From Sand Creek"

GRIN Verlag

Bibliografische Information der Deutschen Nationalbibliothek:

Die Deutsche Bibliothek verzeichnet diese Publikation in der Deutschen National-
bibliografie; detaillierte bibliografische Daten sind im Internet über http://dnb.d-
nb.de/ abrufbar.

Imprint:

Copyright © 2011 GRIN Verlag GmbH
Druck und Bindung: Books on Demand GmbH, Norderstedt Germany
ISBN: 978-3-656-46707-6

This book at GRIN:

http://www.grin.com/en/e-book/230264/native-genocide-and-american-imperialism-
in-simon-ortiz-s-poem-from-sand

GRIN - Your knowledge has value

Der GRIN Verlag publiziert seit 1998 wissenschaftliche Arbeiten von Studenten, Hochschullehrern und anderen Akademikern als eBook und gedrucktes Buch. Die Verlagswebsite www.grin.com ist die ideale Plattform zur Veröffentlichung von Hausarbeiten, Abschlussarbeiten, wissenschaftlichen Aufsätzen, Dissertationen und Fachbüchern.

Visit us on the internet:

http://www.grin.com/

http://www.facebook.com/grincom

http://www.twitter.com/grin_com

Native Genocide and American Imperialism in Simon Ortiz's poem *From Sand Creek*

The late cultural critic Neil Postman spoke frequently about the tendency of technology to become mythic, or accepted without question as something that always existed in the natural world. The same can be said of territorial boundaries, a manmade construct that had no relevance for the Cheyenne and Arapaho people of the foothills and high plains of east of the Rocky Mountains in the mid-19th century. By the latter 20th century, however, the more than two million residents of the state of Colorado who lived amidst the arbitrary demarcation lines of a state without natural boundaries felt a strong enough affinity for and identity with their place in the world to honor, grieve and demand action over the "XXXX number of Coloradoans… killed in Vietnam," or, "…on the highways." (Ortiz 15) Little more than one hundred years earlier, however, several indigenous tribes had thriving and venerable societies that were destroyed by American troops, and like most non-native residents of the United States, the typical Coloradoan had no concern for this fact. "Repression works like shadow, clouding memory and sometimes even to blind, and when it is on a national scale, it is just not good." (Ortiz 14)

Like the white settlers who ultimately forced them out of the territory in the years following the Sand Creek Massacre of 1864, the Cheyenne and Arapaho were not natives of the regions within modern-day Colorado. The Arapaho are believed to have originated near the Red River, and French trappers in what became Chicago evidently traded with the Cheyenne in the 17th century. (Waldman 146-47) Driven west by both rival tribes and white encroachment, the Arapaho and Cheyenne adapted to the new environment and relied heavily on plentiful buffalo for subsistence. They lived mostly unmolested while the territory was claimed by Spain and Mexico. After the territory was acquired by the United States following the Mexican-American War however, prospectors heading to California during the Gold Rush of 1848-49 had modest success panning for gold in the South Platte River Valley. The first treaty with the American government followed shortly thereafter in 1851: it allowed the American government to establish military outposts and roads throughout the region and purported to assure the tribes' rights to, "hunt(ing), fish(ing), or pass(ing) over any of the tracts of country heretofore described." (Brown 68) A major gold strike at Pike's Peak in 1858 brought upwards of 30,000 white prospectors to the area, and the tribes were misled into signing a treaty that confined them to an area around Sand Creek. Confined to unirrigated land that was not suitable for agriculture, they were also restricted from hunting buffalo in the traditional areas in consideration of the soon-to-be-constructed railroad. Led by the chief Black Kettle, the Arapaho managed to survive by hunting in areas still unencroached upon by white settlers or military operations, a feat that was more difficult with each passing year. Even after the chief Lean Bear was in May 1864 shot dead by American soldiers as he approached them unarmed and waving an American flag, Black Kettle conducted frenetic diplomatic talks with fellow chiefs and government troops in favor of peace, finally securing a meeting with Governor John Evans, which was also attended by Col. John Chivington, in late September.

Evans was cold, hostile, and non-committal during the meeting. The Colorado territory was little more than three years old, officially recognized by the lame duck Congress and President after existing for three years as the extralegal territory of Jefferson. In addition to fears that his recent reports to Washington would seem alarmist and without credibility if he accepted Black Kettle's pleas for peace, Evans was keenly aware that many of the newly enlisted short-term Third Colorado Regiment volunteers under Chivington (who called themselves 'hundred dazers') wanted to, "avoid the military draft of 1864 by serving in uniform against a few poorly armed Indians than against the Confederates further east." (Brown 79) The Cheyenne and Arapaho returned to Sand Creek without a peace agreement. On November 5th, Maj. Edward Wynkoop was accused of, "letting the Indians run things at Fort Lyon," and relieved of his command. His replacement was Maj. Scott Anthony, a protégée of Chivington, who drastically reduced the Arapaho's rations and ordered them to surrender all weapons to his soldiers. (Brown 83) The tribes considered slipping away further south, but upon their first meeting Anthony heartily encouraged Black Kettle to stay at Sand Creek for the winter and send his braves away to hunt buffalo until he could secure additional rations for them. (Brown 84) When Chivington and Anthony swept through the Cheyenne and Arapaho encampment the morning of November 29th, most men of

2

fighting age were away, and the remaining populace was unarmed. The 700 mounted troops supported by four howitzers killed 105 women and children and 28 men. Allegedly, many of the participating troops were drunk. A significant number scalped and sexually mutilated the corpses of those they had killed.

Though Chivington and the non-native populace of the Colorado Territory initially saw the massacre as a great victory achieved by brave soldiers, eyewitness accounts from survivors and Army officers like Capt. Silas Soule, Lt. Joseph Campbell, and Lt. James Connor were impassioned enough to gain attention in the halls of Congress. The massacre was investigated by the Joint Committee on the Conduct of the War, a special committee that concerned itself with oversight of the Union effort against the Confederacy that was chaired by Radical Republican Senator Benjamin Wade. Though the committee reprimanded Chivington and recommended that he face a court martial, he and his subordinates escaped punishment. There was no justice whatsoever for the victims: indeed, the remainder of the Arapaho and Cheyenne population were killed or driven from the Colorado territory by October 1865. The actions against these tribes is viewed as the catalyst of the entire campaign against the various tribes of the Great Plains that reached a nadir in another massacre, this time against hundreds of unarmed Lakota Ghost Dancers at Wounded Knee, South Dakota, in 1890.

In this poem and throughout *From Sand Creek*, Ortiz strongly implies that the same impulses that led to the Sand Creek Massacre influenced other atrocities committed by representatives of the American establishment. "Remember My Lai," he says in the poem, citing the most widely known massacre of civilians committed by American troops in Vietnam (Ortiz 15). "When the frontier was declared officially closed in 1890 it was only a short time before American imperialistic impulses drove the country into the Spanish-American War and the acquisition of America's Pacific island empire began" (Deloria 51). Col. Jacob Smith's now-forgotten order to "kill everyone over ten (years old)," during the Samar campaign in the Philippines in 1902 was chillingly reminiscent of Col. Chivington's justification for killing Cheyenne and Arapaho children: "nits make lice." (Brown 73) (Like Chivington, Smith was reprimanded but never charged with a crime.) Deloria ruefully noted in the late 1960s that the prime public justification for

American presence in Vietnam was to maintain faith in the United States' promises, but that, "America has yet to keep one Indian treaty or agreement" of the over 400 that were signed. (Deloria 28)

"It wasn't only the Senators," who forgot, Ortiz says. (Ortiz 15) In 1909, a group called the Colorado Pioneers Association erected a statue on the west steps of the state capitol building putatively honoring Colorado Civil War casualties. The statue's plaque includes the names of soldiers of the Third Colorado Regiment killed by friendly fire during the Sand Creek Massacre, and characterizes their deaths as having occurred during a battle. "In fifty years, nobody knew what happened." (Ortiz 15) As a result of this national repression, in the historical consciousness of the mainstream American, "In 1864, there were no Indians killed." (Ortiz 15)

Ortiz ends the poem with an admonition to, "Remember Sand Creek" (Ortiz 15). Yet the historical repression in both Colorado and the United States as a whole remains in the present day, despite the best efforts of scholars and poets like Ortiz.

Works Cited

Brown, Dee. *Bury My Heart at Wounded Knee: An Indian History of the American West* New York: Holt, Rinehart and Winston, 1970. Second printing.

Deloria, Vine, *Custer Died For Your Sins*. Norman, Oklahoma: University of Oklahoma Press, 1988.

Ortiz, Simon J. *From Sand Creek* Tucson: University of Arizona Press, 2000.

Waldman, Carl. *Atlas of the North American Indian* New York: Facts of File, 1985.